A Piece of America's Heart

Poems by Tony Moffeit

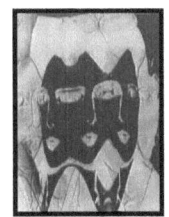

Casa de Cinco
Hermanas Press,
Pueblo, CO

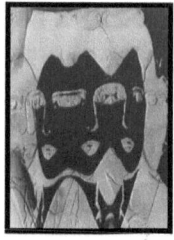

Copyright © Tony Moffeit, 2024
First Edition: 1 3 5 7 9 10 8 6 4 2
ISBN: 978-1-952411-95-3
LCCN: 2022932786

Cover image: Tony Moffeit
Author photo: Freeman Crocker
All rights reserved. No part of this publication may be reproduced or transmitted in any form or by any means, electronic or mechanical, including photocopying, recording or by info retrieval system, without prior written permission from the author.

Acknowledgments:

Grateful acknowledgment to the following publications where these poems first appeared, some in other versions and under different titles:

Casa de Cinco Hermanas: "Highways, Mountains, Rivers, Blood," "Mexican Music and a Rooster Crowing," "Taking the Road," *Cholla Needles:* "Do You Believe," *Last Call, Chinaski* (Lummox Press anthology): "Been Here and Gone," *Lummox:* "I Am the Poem Never Written," "I Have Learned to Sleep and Dream Songs," "Tattoos Don't Cover All the Scars," "A Woman With No Arms," *Malpais Review:* "It Was the Last Night for the Blues," "Shapeshifter," "Searching for Pedro," *Midnight Train to Dodge* (Pueblo Poetry Project anthology): "Down a Crooked Street," "Faces Ride the Train," "Midnight Tarot," *Waymark:* "Birds Out of Smoke," "Channeling the Blues," "Learning How to Breathe Again," "Metamorphosis," "The Night It Rained the Blues," "Running Deep," "Silhouette," "The Space You Occupy," "Turning Back," "You Are Here," "A Woman With No Arms," "Flamenco Dancing," "My Eye Is You,"

"Relentless" previously appeared in the chapbook *Barroom Ballads & Merle Haggard Blues.*

Table of Contents

Looking for the Black Bird

Highways, Mountains, Rivers, Blood / 1
The Night It Rained the Blues / 5
Equinox / 6

Catch a Whisper of Light

Faces Ride the Train / 11
Mexican Music and a Rooster Crowing / 12
Taking the Road / 14
Relentless / 16
Birds Out of Smoke / 18
Been Here and Gone / 19
Searching for Pedro / 21
You Are Here / 22

No Souvenirs

Learning How To Breathe Again / 27
Shapeshifter / 28
Silhouette / 31
The Space You Occupy / 33
Metamorphosis / 34
Ghosts of New Orleans / 35
At First Sight / 37
It Was the Last Night for the Blues / 38

A Silence to Your Eyes

Turning Back / 45
A Woman With No Arms / 46
Midnight Tarot / 48
Down a Crooked Street / 49
Tattoos Don't Cover All the Scars / 50
When the Time Comes / 52
Night Wolf / 53
I Have Learned to Sleep and Dream Songs / 55

Bones Beating Together

Do You Believe / 61
My Eye Is You / 62
Running Deep / 64
Channeling the Blues / 65
Rush of Fever / 67
I Am the Poem Never Written / 70

A PIECE OF AMERICA'S HEART

Looking for the Black Bird

Highways, Mountains, Rivers, Blood

i want to tell you about
america

i want to tell you about
saturday night neon and
street corner singers

i want to tell you about
small town carnivals
and tunnels of love
backdoors and kitchens
forests and rivers
drive-in movies
and salvage yards
steel mill fire

i want to tell you
about america

i want to tell you
about old songs and dirt roads
strangers meeting just once
and that is enough
out of a dream and into a song

the pain caught in the lyrics
of hank williams

the blues felt in the voice
of robert johnson

let me sing
let me moan
let me shout
spirits working their way
through sleep
for bodies broken
and mended again
a line
thrown aside on a
street corner
the metaphor the archetype
the myth the legend
the symbol the sign the signal

let me tell you about
a frame-up a conspiracy
a tall tale a mad diary
a nocturne a lullaby
a midnight blues

let me tell you about
a souvenir a fetish a totem
a siren a train whistle
a church bell

i want to tell you
about the cat trying to move in

about the tramp wanting a ride
about the deer
on the side of the road

let me sing
of las vegas, san antonio,
new orleans
let me sing
of billy the kid
marie laveau
endless skies
and endless roads

i want to tell you about
sprawling highway jams
and makeshift graves
off the side of the road
manikins in windows
art galleries bookstores
houses hidden with a
view of the mountains

let me tell you about
a line from a movie
a line from a song
the night itching
with madness
the bars the rivers
the honky tonks

let me tell you about
the blasting of songs
and shouts and wild screams
and in the distance
the silence of mountains

the years have circled back
on themselves
the alleyways reverberate
with the blues
jazz plays out
as the lights change

caught up in the endless traffic
of the full moon shining
and the pull of the tides
fiddles and steel guitars
take the high road
someone wanting
the ghost of a chance
someone else taking
the ribbon of the highway
everyone agreeing on
the speed of a falling star

The Night It Rained the Blues

all that matters
is what i cannot say
the message of eyes
transferred from
one person to another
so that a glance
becomes a voice
a voice becomes a word
a word becomes a phrase
a phrase becomes
an embrace
the phantom saxophone
that blows a pain
that cannot be too great
the body a blues
falling down like rain
how far you have to go
to get at the roots of things
the way a certain angle of light
conquers space
the shapes not as important
as the entering by chance
of something that is
as spontaneous as jazz
or the images of a silent movie
to evoke without speech
the intimacy
of fingers on a back

Equinox

a frontier mapped out
by heroes and villains
why the world is structured as it is
and how it works
people think this is the world but it isn't
the world is a bubble a fantasy
greater than reality
a cigarette thrown on the ground
by bogart in the maltese falcon
and eyes that peer
through the fog
looking for the black bird

the poem as much a part of us
as the breath the sweat
the appetite
a movie of our life
with scenes and dialogue
a stream of consciousness
and unconsciousness
heart jumping through throat
the healer in his trance
attention to the breath

the evanescence
we're here for a little while
and then we're gone

another spring
the secret is in stretching
the moment
transcending time
using space as a vehicle

the image stolen
made immortal by
the lust for it
the image
set up
as a scat song
a riff
to see yourself framed
in negative
colors reversed
secrets revealed
as you listen
with eyes closed
as if you can hear
the colors of sound
equinox
and an hour
of light
stolen from the darkness
a solo of sleep
the day before yesterday
filtered through to
the day after tomorrow

Catch a Whisper of Light

Faces Ride the Train

a piece of american art you could tell
there was blood on the canvas
the blood of hell there was a
hound howling it was a piece of
american art it had gone too far
there were faces on the wall
faces on the train it was a piece
of american art you could tell
billy the kid was in there
there were faces everywhere
the woman of the black bayou
the speed of the rockabilly rebel
the renegade rocker was
casting a spell the velocity
of it all a conjure mix raw and wild
the canvas was on fire yes
the neon was singing a backstreet
blues o yeah a piece of america
art is dangerous o yeah
everything and nothing that's
what it's all about it's everything
in nothing and a rebel yell
a piece of american art
it's as if the body can't hold it
it's gotta get out cut up the canvas
american mask made of paper
that's what art is all about
you burn you turn you bend you fall
in the desperado night of it all

Mexican Music and
a Rooster Crowing

there is a new cat
sleeping on my front porch
there is a new dog
barking in my backyard
there are yard sales
and ice cream trucks
on my block
at night a lonesome
whistle blows
in the morning the
rooster crows in the alley
there is mexican music
coming from my
neighbor's house
i keep my old mars red
camaro parked out front
never drive it because
it is just a piece of
sculpture although
my neighbors want to
buy it and use it as
a car again the
insurance payments
are driving me nuts

but still i refuse to sell
my newspapers pile up
on my front porch the
u.s. mail clogs my
mailbox and the weeds
are growing through
my rocks i won't even
begin to describe the
interior of my house
my neighbors try to
peek in to get a glimpse
of chaos all they know
about me is that i give
performances, of what,
they have no idea, but
are still waiting for
an invitation

Taking the Road

i'm taking the road to the sky
the highway to the horizon
reality is only a state of mind
clouds which slide into mountains
wind and adobe
dust tumbleweed and stucco
the cries of birds from the hills
are my songs or the healing
that takes place when words arrive
like lightning before a storm
the space between the eyes
knocking on the door of time
taking dictation from a distant star
the dead speak to me through poems
like animals uncaged
like a bridge to some
invisible landscape
leaving a heiroglyph
for some future life
targeted on this planet
a mosaic of flesh and bones
let me paint the ravine
with the blood of dreams
out of the corner of my eye
let me catch a whisper of light

that runs like a river
through your spine
let the journey continue
in the ritual of wind and rain
bring the sky inside

Relentless

i wanted to tell you something
now i can't even remember what it was
a phrase, a song title, i think
something i knew i would never forget
then i forgot it
something about love and death
something about being buried alive
something about the loss of love
as being buried alive
something merle haggard could have sung
an outlaw's music
wrapped up in the pain of love
it's the only way to get even
a horse called retribution
ridden on the prairie of night
and now i'm looking for something
but i don't know what i'm looking for
maybe a word maybe a sign
maybe a signal
something that sings in the night
something that rings in the mountains
let me sleep on the wind
let me learn how to breathe again
i'll know it when i see it
out of a need to be born to it

those accidental phrases
archetypes hidden in asides
secret weapons
from those who give you back
to yourself

Birds Out of Smoke

helgoe painted his skin white
said it was a moment of clarity
and on the way to the hospital
said this time i know i'm right
i've been wrong so many times

helgoe painted birds coming
out of smoke on the prairie
buffaloes formed from sun
in the desert and pilot owls
guiding spacemen on the plains

but when he filled his pores
with white paint so they
could no longer breathe he knew
at once that this bones' singing
was his greatest masterpiece

Been Here and Gone

i hear the sound of
garbage trucks in the
alley dawn collecting
the trash of my
discarded poems
and the fractured cars
outside my house
are sculptures for
a retired steel worker
the beer is good
the game is fast
and the risk won't last
but to be born again
is all you can ask
to whittle the words
with the language
of knives
words as fractured
as the cars to be
sculpted and shined
or left to rust
in a junkyard of time
or born again
with new tires
with new lights

i'll take that
crevice of light
from moving metal
along highways
of second-hand lives

Searching for Pedro

the zen masters speak of the
nothingness before birth and
after death and so it is the
great void i think of when
listening to lou reed sing
"some kinda love" a rhythm
a pulse a beat sliding into
the veins like a piece of
invisibility la dee ta ta ta
a barrage of guitars proving
there is no intensity better
than detachment picking up
a sound based in a higher
mathematics of substance
equals void like a bum
racing out of the no name
bar shouting hey pedro
hey pedro and running
across the street to the
train station looking for
the invisible pedro
when i ask a woman
what is going on
she replies i'm tired of
having all the answers

You Are Here

i was the mathematician
who told you one plus one equals one
but your equation was even simpler
you must reject me to accept me
danger was a part of the equation
as was forever
and the risks ahead
several lifetimes yet to be lived
in a search for an ecstasy
that is sweeter than death
found in the gutcry of the blues
or the image seen just once
but never forgotten
caught by a camera
in the flash of an instant
releasing a spirit into the air
an air we are still learning
how to breathe
words we are still
learning how to speak
deciphering the syllables
as if numbers to an equation
or the latest artifacts
to be auctioned from
the possession of
the estate of a living legend
as pure as the cigarette

dangling from the mouth
of the early western star
as he sits atop his horse

No Souvenirs

Learning How to Breathe Again

and there is nothing left
the world has been blown to bits
no space no time no perception
maybe just one drop of water
maybe just one charge of fire
to start anew
something to be created out of nothing
the vague semblance of language
the void creating itself out of the void
one thought tilting a constellation
the makings of a consciousness
born birth born
all the nights
all the eyes
the cold is so warm
in the heat of the road
let me be
i'll work it all out by myself
learning how to breathe again
do you believe me now
substance giving way to expression
a piece of space to work through
a sliver of light
a parcel of sound
and the crossings

Shapeshifter

miles runs the voodoo down
blows smoke rings with his horn
turns time circular
shapeshifter of death moan
sickness as a path to great health
finding the space of silence
finding a new equation
streetcorner celebration
miles runs the voodoo down
what are you practicing these days?
i'm practicing life
no death no past no history
shapeshifter what are you teaching
these days?
i'm teaching immortality
and what about the secret of sleep?
ah yes that too
inventing your own dreams
changing the temperature
with your thoughts
sleepwalk ghost walk floating
above your bed
shapeshifter levitating your body
to your own kind of blues
automatic writing automatic solo
are you creating a deathmask?
ah the flame is strong

scorching fire for the deathmask
i saw his ghost in my driveway
over by the trashcan
it's more than electronics
it's more than a tape recording
of the dead
shapeshifter of language
your own kind of blues
miles runs the voodoo down
desert coyote
shapeshifter of bones
to level the playing field
after all
it is what it is
something to provide balance
a chaos to provide balance
a new riff for
dancing in the dark
staccato cactus type of blues
death was never in the equation
is it possible to find
beyond the tombstone
celebration
or in the special angle
of the moment
the lingering phantom breath?
miles runs the voodoo down
learning to tranquilize the arms
the legs
what is this dialogue?

out of the past
a way to darkness
red tide
before birth
there is great laughter
after death
there is great laughter
ah the great mirage
for your desert horn
fractured
summon the shapes
shapeshifter
and run

Silhouette

silent
under a howling moon
all i have left
from lost highways
are the scars
of barroom songs
a shadow seeking
a shadow
like a penitente
carrying a cross
on his back
the only way
to a miracle
through pain
washed in the blood
of a moon
and the lyrics
to the blues
the future
begging the past
to let go
the past seeking
its imprint
on the future
through the shadow
of a whisper
a symbol

an archetype
a mask for a
new identity
twin of your
former self

The Space You Occupy

i set my clocks fifteen minutes fast
to live in the future as much as the past

i'll take anything you can give me
like the ghost of a chance

i was made for wide open spaces
the distance that brings you closer

there's a flier in my mailbox
left by the pony express

voice in search of a body
face in search of a mask

Metamorphosis

was it a victory
or the transcendence
of defeat
eyes no longer there
mouths no longer there
as we sit together
at ringside
the gladiators we watch
are ourselves
eyes replaced by eye black
to reduce the glare
mouths replaced by
the roar of the crowd
vibrations exchanged
from the fog of cages
out of sleep
come our second shadows
our second selves
if i could only find
your reflection
a hint of your identity
in the wind
visiting our skin

Ghosts of New Orleans

thunder and the dance of lightning
the ghosts of new orleans
taken from the rain
we walk pirates alley
in a wind of jinx and juju
shoulder to shoulder with marie
and a snake called zombi
i hear a drum on rue royale
a washboard on rue bourbon
the rhythms get into my fingers
the beat gets into my feet
it's those ghosts of new orleans
taken from a dream

on a french quarter balcony
we howl to a midnight blues
with a chorus of ghosts behind us
chanting jazz
every word a kiss
every phrase an embrace
it's as easy as one two three
the ghosts of new orleans
taken from a grave

let's do a spell of chicken voodoo
mix a bag of gris gris
throw the hex out on the street

where we drive in a mojomobile
there's a book in the backroom
with the secrets of haiti
the ghosts of new orleans
know those secrets o so well

o those ghosts of new orleans
taken from the rain
as we splash in the streets and sidewalks
to the streetcalls supreme
hey you hey blue
hey oysters on the half shell
we stride in midnight streets
do a hand jive called
the snake chain to the ghosts
the ghosts of new orleans

At First Sight

i've already forgotten the future
        and the night dance of spiders

the light is stealing
                an hour from
                the darkness
the earth
        the rocks
                the shadows
        the rain-stretched wind
        the rain-drenched roof
thunder
                my lightning eyes
the shift of a train
        to nowhere

a voice no longer concealed
but carried out into the storm

the dark sleep of a pulsing street

and now you're gone
        look what you left behind

It Was the Last Night for the Blues

and it is the sweat that becomes an ocean
and it is the tear that becomes a river
and it is the breath that becomes a hurricane
and it is the blood that becomes a tornado
and there is a dark tide that creeps up on you
as you drive the dark mountains of colorado
as you drive the dark road under a voodoo moon
as you drive the wailing darkness into boulder
and the television tells you of the last night for the blues
and you know it was the last night
the last night at the end of the universe
the last night for the crescent city
the last night for the big easy
it was the last night for the blues

before the night before the rain before the dawn
before the dusk before the words before the notes
before the living before the dying before the blood
before the skin before the bones before the breath
before the laughing before the drinking before the
sleeping before the waking there is love no souvenirs
there is love no souvenirs

it was the last night for the blues
it was the last night for the blues

the city went down
the levee went down
the city went down
the levee went down

it was the last night for the blues
it was the last night for the blues

and when there is death everywhere
there is love no souvenirs
and when there is displacement everywhere
there is love no souvenirs
and when there is isolation everywhere
there is love no souvenirs
and when it is the last night for the blues
there is love no souvenirs

give me mojo, mama, ain't got no home
give me juju, mama, can't find my mind
it was the last night
give me mojo, mama, ain't got no home
give me juju, mama, can't find my mind
it was the last night

it was the last night for the blues
it was the last night for the blues

let me drive through the mountains
let me blast through the blackness of 1 a.m.

let me reach a bluesmoan of a moon
let me reach out and touch the water of stars
let me leap out into space where the moon
pulls the tide of the blood
let me drive through the mountains
where the road is so black
you can barely make out the curves the turns
where the headlights are beacons
of a telepathic lighthouse
and my saliva has become a taste of the flood

the city went down
the levee went down

it was the last night for the blues
it was the last night for the blues

and spirit is everywhere
in the midst of life and death
and you can take it anywhere
in the midst of life and death
and the ghosts are everywhere
in the midst of life and death
and you can talk with the ghosts
in the midst of life and death
and you can dance with the ghosts
in the midst of life and death
and there is love no souvenirs
in the midst of life and death
for everything is gone

in the midst of life and death
everything dissolves
in the midst of life and death
everything but love
in the midst of life and death

it was the last night
and all the clocks turned to wails that night
it was the last night
and all the mirrors reflected ghosts that night
it was the last night
and i drove a long and desolate road that night
it was the last night
and the moon pulled the sweat from the body
it was the last night
and the body became a bayou that night
it was the last night
it was the last night
it was the last night for the blues

A Silence to Your Eyes

Turning Back

the voices outside cannot be understood
but a rhythm travels under the door
the secrets still inhabited in a suitcase
in a space that conjures change
the door opens once again
and the colors are released
there is sound there is sweat
there are footsteps down a hall
there is a story never told anymore
there are vibrations of a whisper
left over from the fire of the desert
hunting something elusive
that passes back in time
at the corner the light changes
those who walk and those who drive
contemplate time earth memory
and it's all dissolving in the intersection
everything is moving in circles
it is time to want everything
even the road back to yourself
nothing anymore forever
everything that happens
where somebody waits

A Woman With No Arms

i am something
and its opposite
i am two
the space beneath the dream
the skeleton of thought
puppets and mirrors and masks
everything is perfect
time is waiting in the wind
i am a woman with no arms
i play the guitar with my feet

i refuse to be broken
fingers of wind palms of sleep
and in their moving a landscape
of hands so today the dust is
moist and there exists a
rhythm that rises like mist
a feeling of bones dissolving
in the earth

i am a woman with no arms
i learned to drive with my feet
what is it we can do
a tongue to speak in
what you want me to do
in the broken down light
to face the night
let's dance on a dark star

i have found the secret
of turning toes
into fingers
reversing
the order of things

i refuse to be broken
like pieces of a mosaic
reassembled again
in a geometry of resurrection

let me hold you
with my invisible arms
a regeneration of love
i seek the impossible

Midnight Tarot

your words filling the air
with a sky of blood when
you have battled all the forces
and hit rock bottom
like an image that doesn't
even know itself anymore
unless it is superimposed
on another the roads are
calling and you can't stop
moving and existence as
always is circular
there is no shadow no mirror
no neoned jukebox to bring
you back only cheese enchiladas
red chile and mexican beer

Down a Crooked Street

perception has become magnified
existence has taken on a new theater
outside has become inside in a hand
a finger a tool for an actor a gunhand
bullet eyes and i have become obsessed
with the menus of restaurants they
speak to me with the visions of their
language foods beers appetizers
and the conversations of people
swoop into my ears like startled birds
ricochet in my brain for an answer
i remember john wesley hardin once
shot and killed a man for snoring
the edges of perception determine
the longevity of vision my movements
have become the machinery of a
new mammal baptized in blood

Tattoos Don't Cover All the Scars

one thing at a time
he said
the large man sitting next to me
on a bench
with his walker and oxygen tank
tattoos running up and down his arms
both of us waiting for rides
it's like dying and coming to life again
every day
he said
i had no idea nor interest
in what he was talking about
and his voice grew louder
as he told me about his afflictions
and i won't tell you what he said
only that he said it
in a loud voice
and he would not stop
i was getting sick to my stomach
listening to assortment after assortment
of ailments procedures rare diseases
and cures worse than diseases
and all i could think was
ride ride please come
but as he shifted into the next tale of his conditions
i thought
i need to concentrate on something else

and channel out his monologue
so i focused on the tattoos
on both his arms covering scars
if you looked closely you
could see the lines of the scars
had become a part of the tattoos
when the man said
one more thing
and it was one of those
moments when you have to choose
between running
or listening to one more line
of an exhausting diatribe
i chose to listen:
i swore that if i ever got this bad
i would take a gun and shoot myself
but now that i'm here
all i care about
is waking up tomorrow

When the Time Comes

the candles we burn
the bells that toll
when the time comes
bring a silence
to your eyes

the breath unveils
secrets of sleep
as mouth asks mouth
as food finds food
and words find words

which is to say
what shape do we take
when the time comes
the dance
the other i become

Night Wolf

i look for openings wild things changes
apache fog an albuquerque low
read the messages the windchime night
everything remaining the same
in order to change the naked grave
when doors close behind me
they will not find me
what is it you have to say
you know just what to do
get into the rhythm this side of you
the shape you choose no time to lose
roll like wild gypsy dice
been down for you
way down for blue
like cat bones that shake
like a love rattle a snake sound
i want the darkness when all the lights
have left the night and there is a
new kind of blood for the bones to
listen to nothing left but the breath
and the hunger you are there and yet
not there wind and dust burning
in your laughter
have you had enough
coming down hard

ain't got a thing
that's the way i like it
shifting in shadows
i'll remain out there
where the whispers lie

I Have Learned to Sleep
and Dream Songs

in the dream i am having a beer
with kell robertson in a cafe
in a small town in new mexico
when a woman approaches our
booth and asks about the black
notebook beside me what do
you have in there? she asks
and i reply my songs and she
inquires further would you
sing one of them? and before
i can answer kell remarks
if you'll join me in my booth,
i'll sing one of them for you
so the woman slides into the
booth beside kell and kell
begins belting out a song that
i am obviously writing in
my dream, it's called "i get
along with you" kell is
singing it acapella no blood
red guitar and every word is
perfect every note is perfect
and the restaurant crowd is
amazed, clapping and singing
along with the chorus "i get
along with you" i am thinking

it can't get any better than this
but it does because the woman
who asked about the song and
joined kell in the booth
miraculously begins
inventing words to the song
begins singing a whole
new verse based on her life
and ending with "that's why
i get along with you" the
restaurant crowd is going nuts
clapping and singing along
with the chorus "that's why
i get along with you" and i'm
thinking it can't get any better
than this but it does because
another woman, two booths
down, takes the song on a
whole new spontaneous
adventure, after kell, after
the first woman, the second
woman belts out a version
based on her life, and ending
with "that's why i get along
with you" and now the song
is no longer my song, no
longer kell's song, no longer
the first woman's song, no
longer the second woman's
song, the song belongs to the

restaurant crowd, belongs to
the people who are yelling
and clapping and repeating
the chorus "that's why i get
along with you" the dream
ends with a shot of kell's face
detached but satisfied as if
to say, i've been dead for
five years but i've still got it

Bones Beating Together

Do You Believe

there was a blackness so mysterious
that even the television set was mystical
white glow of a pale rider on horseback
never was there a blackness this black
the white glow of his face when he
met a lady by the river on the screen
the room jet black
and their bodies luminous
all was liquid all was wet and shimmering
and in the blackness
the television glowed like a new god

do you believe in first sight
the white glow in the black room
the remote to the television:
forward rewind record
and my favorite: pause
so that if you fall in love
with something at first sight
you can freeze the image

My Eye Is You

let me leave my ghost words
like petroglyphs
in the slurred syllables
of a blues song
my ears are my own
let me beat my drum
i am born in you
like the pigeons that
return to my roof
i have staying power
as i listen to them
mumble like method actors
living out their lines
the delicate balance of things
like merle haggard
hanging on by a thread
then letting go
only merle could pull off
dying on his birthday
reminding us he was
born in a boxcar
in bakersfield
my eye is you
don't you know my hands
i speak to you
with lips closed
trying to find a signal

an image a message
in words on paper
scratched out in an
isolated junkyard
in a landscape
of train tracks
so i can hear the
whistle blow the
rhythm of life and
death the lonesome
whistle of merle
haggard of johnny cash
of prisons and
escapes from prisons
of the essence of things
and the opposites
transcendence
of opposites
life death
imprisonment freedom
who am i
i am the nothingness
out of which comes
everything
the broken bottle
of tequila
in a ditch on
the side of the road
glistening in the sun

Running Deep

the breeze lingers just long enough
to answer all the questions of midnight
thought forms grains of consciousness
the skeleton of memory
like a tremor of earthquake
something born out of idea matter
wash yourself in sound
move in circles
the eyes can see again
the rhythm of bones beating together
i was there between worlds
in order to seek a space
i will be there over time
between worlds destinations visions
to improvise the echoes of an unknown wheel
a move a mood
i would like to find the window to enter
the skull and the spine
the shape of the flame
the mirror of the dice
all the way down the line
to seek what is left
of the wheel of time
mysterious ruins
abandoned mines

Channeling the Blues

in order to prove the gun was not loaded
johnny ace put the gun to his temple

and pulled the trigger
christmas day1954 in houston

and the words of his song were on
everyone's lips like an invisible kiss

just let me love you tonight
forget about tomorrow

and it was like a total eclipse
seen by early man discovering

a new way of revealing heat
or the importance of

the evolution of the thumb
johnny ace chanting

never let me go as if a little piece
of immortality could be defined

by a rhythm and blues singer
on a 45 played over and over

an endless refrain born anew
a channeling of the blues

time lost on the horizon
where darkness yields a new light

like the first sun when water
appeared on a parched earth

Rush of Fever

from new orleans
down the mississippi river
float my bones
and painted skull
souvenirs of the blues
my body has become
the amulets and charms
fetishes and spells
of voodoo

give me what you seek
give me what has been set into motion
give me the form you will become
defined by a name
i'll take anything you can give me
the night the rain the dream
the landscape of a face
the architecture of an eye a hand
the shoulder from behind
so that even now
the truth the real
can be an optical illusion

i'm looking for something
i can't even remember losing

what was it
now i know
improvisation
the extension of saturday night
into sunday morning

the fading of december
into january
spontaneous regeneration
how else could you play
the trickster
without trying
read the eyes of the haunted one
hear the cries
a tongue to speak in
return to you
return to who you are

we crave the perfect balance
of heat and light
come into the wild
with the breath the sweat
the appetite
as if one image
is enough to make a difference

i want to sing a poem
but i cannot find my voice
can only give to you
something like a

low chant
fading into a whisper
it's only the words
which have a strength
not my voice
worn down by
a body seeking
the only blood
it has left

I Am the Poem Never Written

i am the poem never written
in the fog of that rainy night
a ghost saxophone blowing
an ancient song and all you
could do was feel your own heartbeat

i am the poem that never got transcribed
the one that was lost to the night
never written down because you knew that
you would never forget it
and then you did

i am the poem that never survived
not even in the faintest whisper
the poem that struggled in your skin
only to leak out of your pores

i am the poem that never came to life
in a flash of lightning was gone
caught between thought and surrender

i am the poem that disappeared before it could dance
under the neon lights of an old motel
where everything is coming undone

i am the poem that burned
in the open wounds of your fire
the heat of your breath disappearing it

i am the poem that ran out of time
when the clock turned to windchimes
by an abandoned church
on the east side

i am the poem that cannot be brought back
even by seances
even by mediums

i am the poem that was left
in the wet fields of sudden rain
where scarecrows dress in tuxedos
and pigs are carried in limos

i am the poem abandoned
left with no clothes
i am the poem naked and alone
i am the poem
searching for survival

i am the poem drowned in a river
tossed from a mountain
thrown from a crashing car
tattered from the wind
or torn from a poet's fingers

i am the poem falling like snow
i am the poem going up in flames
i am the poem that cannot be saved

Tony Moffeit is the co-founder, along with Todd Moore, of the Outlaw Poetry Movement. His book of essays and poems, POETRY IS DANGEROUS, THE POET IS AN OUTLAW, a volume from Floating Island Publications, is an early delineation of Outlaw Poetry. Moffeit was the winner of the Jack Kerouac Award from Cherry Valley Editions, Cherry Valley, New York, for his volume of poetry, PUEBLO BLUES. He was the recipient of a National Endowment for the Arts creative writing fellowship in 1992.

www.ingramcontent.com/pod-product-compliance
Lightning Source LLC
Chambersburg PA
CBHW060538080526
44586CB00012B/792